Biggest,

Strongest,

Fastest

by Steve Jenkins

Houghton Mifflin Company
Boston

For Robin

Bibliography

Bateman, Graham (ed). *Children's Encyclopedia of the Animal Kingdom*. New York: Dorset, 1991.
Buchsbaum, Ralph, et al.. *The National Audubon Society of Animal Life*. New York: Clarkson N. Potter, 1982.
De Carli, Franco. *The World of Fish*. New York: Abbeville Press, 1975.
Morris, Rick. *Mysteries & Marvels of Ocean Life*. London: Usborne Publishing Limited, 1983.
Taylor, Barbara. *The Animal Atlas*. London: Dorling Kindersley Limited, 1992.

Printed in Singapore

Book design by Steve Jenkins
The text of this book is set in 20 point Century Old Style.
The illustrations are paper collage, reproduced in full color.

TWP   30 29 28 27 26 25 24

Library of Congress Cataloging-in-Publication Data
Jenkins, Steve.   Biggest, strongest, fastest / by Steve Jenkins.   p.   cm.
Includes bibliographic references   RNF ISBN 0-395-69701-8   PAP ISBN 0-395-86136-5
1. Animals—Miscellanea—Juvenile literature. [1. Animals—Miscellanea.]
I. Title.   QL49.J45 1995 591—dc20   94-21804   CIP AC

Animals live all around us. They crawl, walk, run, hop, swim, and fly. Some animals are too small to see without a microscope. Others, like the blue whale, are bigger than a house. There are animals that move as fast as a car and animals that would need half an hour to cross a room.

Here are some of the biggest and smallest, fastest and slowest, strongest and longest animals. They are the record holders of the animal world.

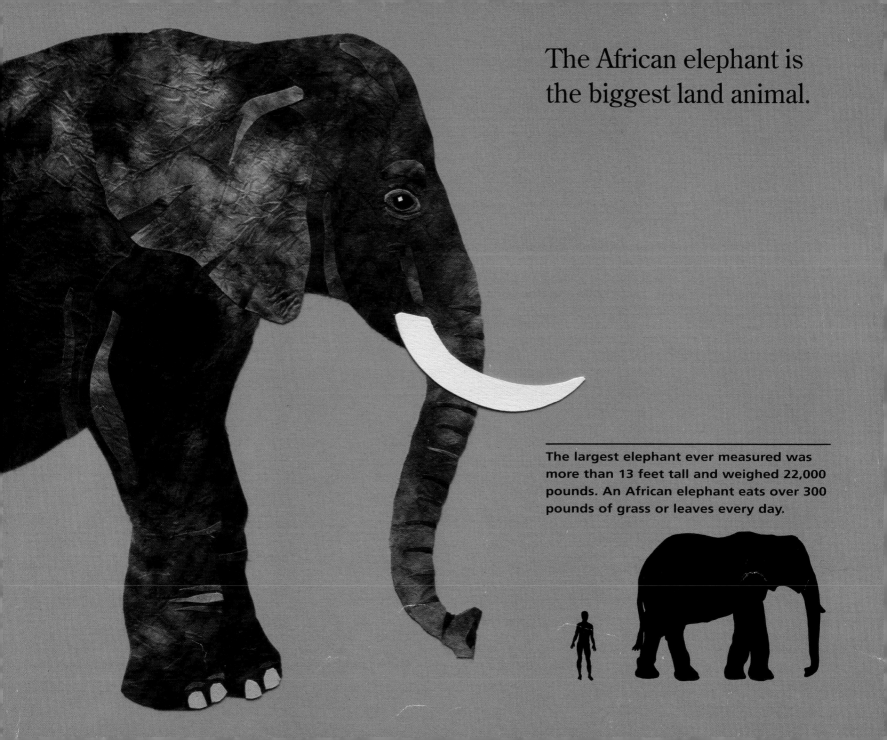

The African elephant is the biggest land animal.

The largest elephant ever measured was more than 13 feet tall and weighed 22,000 pounds. An African elephant eats over 300 pounds of grass or leaves every day.

The strongest animal,
for its size, is the ant.

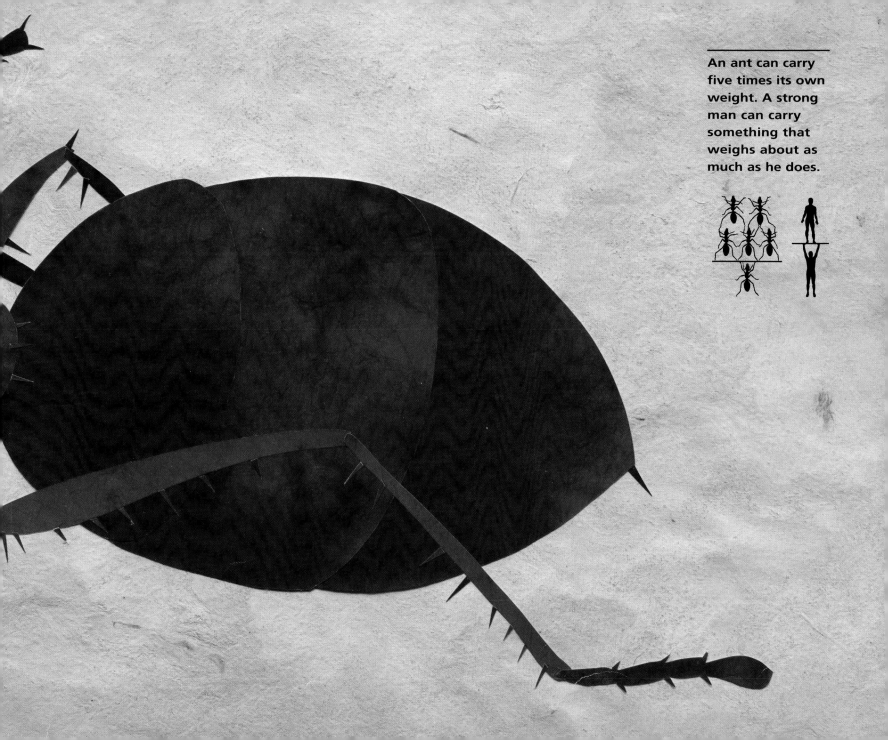

An ant can carry
five times its own
weight. A strong
man can carry
something that
weighs about as
much as he does.

The tallest animal is the giraffe.

Male giraffes grow as tall as 19 feet; the females are a little shorter. With their great height and long, flexible necks, giraffes can eat leaves that other grazing animals cannot reach.

The blue whale

is the biggest animal

that has ever lived.

A blue whale can grow to be 110 feet long
and weigh over 168 tons — as much as 20
elephants. Even the biggest dinosaur was
smaller than a blue whale.

The Etruscan shrew, the world's smallest mammal, could sleep in a teaspoon.

From the tip of its nose to the end of its tail, this shrew is only 2 1/2 inches long. It weighs about as much as a Ping-Pong ball.

The smallest bird is the
bee hummingbird.

The bee hummingbird
is an acrobatic flier
that is only 3 inches
long. It weighs 1/30
of an ounce — less
than a dime.

The sun jellyfish

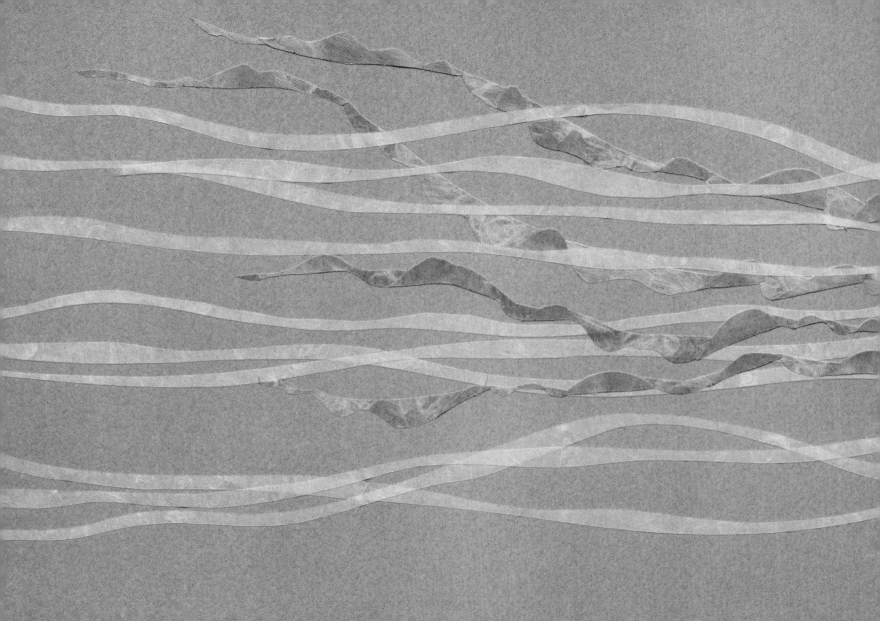

is the world's longest animal.

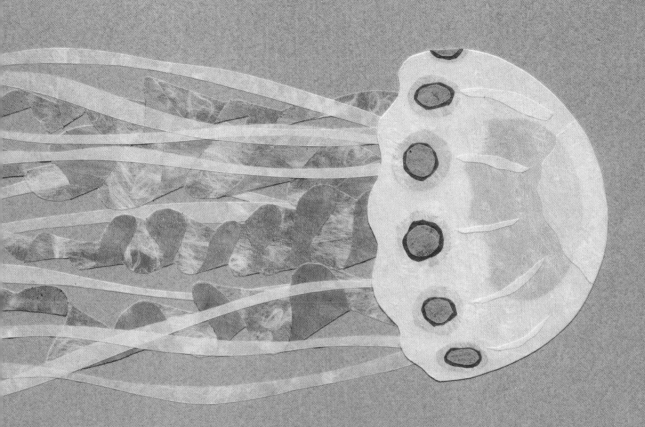

Sun jellyfish have tentacles over 200 feet long. They drag these poisonous filaments through the water to stun fish, which they then catch and eat.

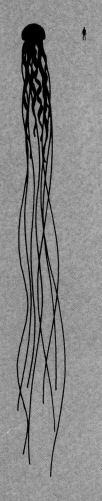

The largest kind of spider is the bird spider.

The bird spider measures almost a foot across and has a poisonous bite. It spins a very strong web to trap the birds and large insects it eats.

The cheetah can run faster than any other animal.

A cheetah can reach speeds of over 60 miles
an hour, but only for a few hundred feet.
When it chases another fast animal, such as
an antelope, the cheetah must catch it quickly.

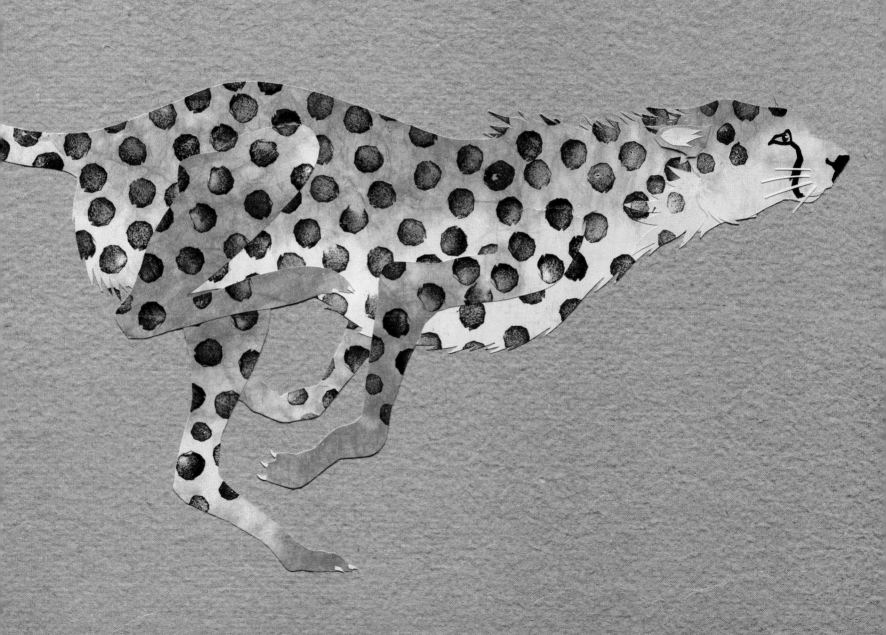

The electric eel
gives the strongest shock
of any animal.

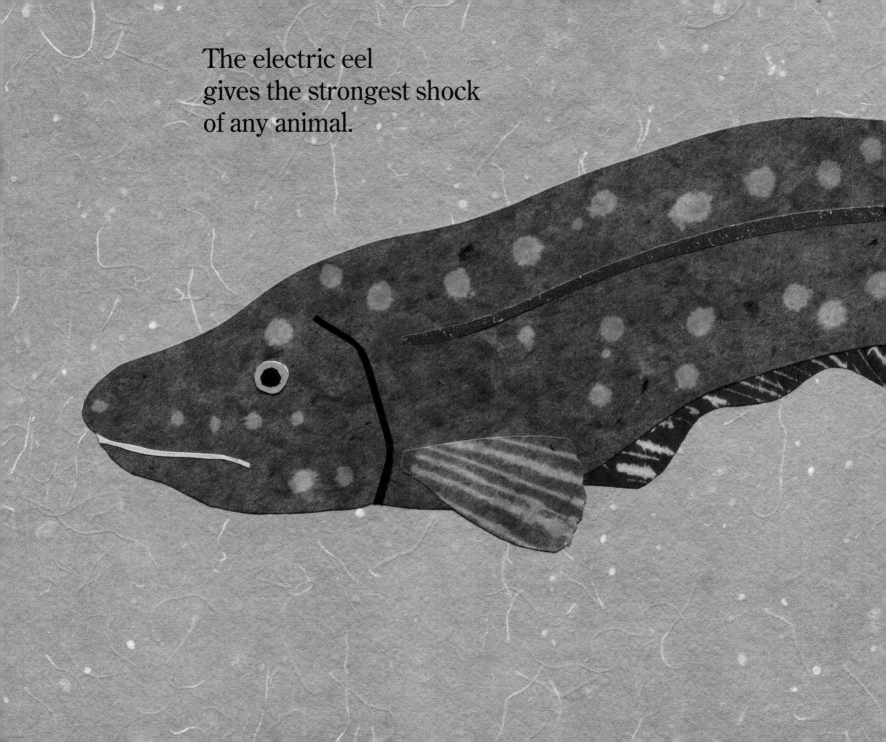

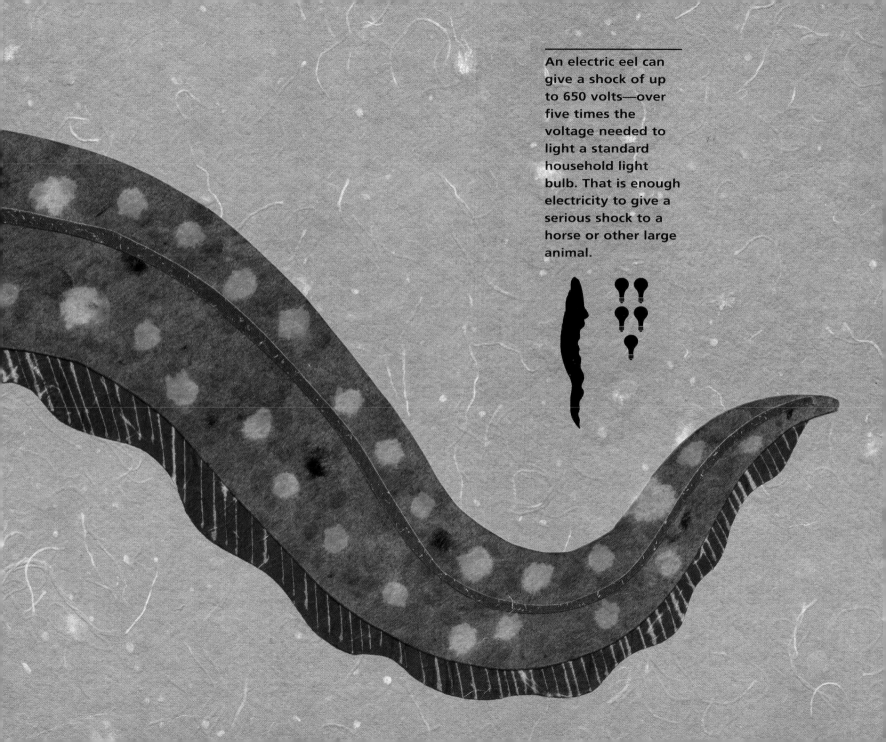

An electric eel can give a shock of up to 650 volts—over five times the voltage needed to light a standard household light bulb. That is enough electricity to give a serious shock to a horse or other large animal.

The land snail is one of the slowest animals.

Some snails can move only 8 inches in a minute. At that speed the snail would need 5 1/2 days to travel one mile. Fortunately the snail, with its hard shell, does not need to run away from danger.

There are
many kinds of
large snakes,
but the
anaconda is
the biggest.

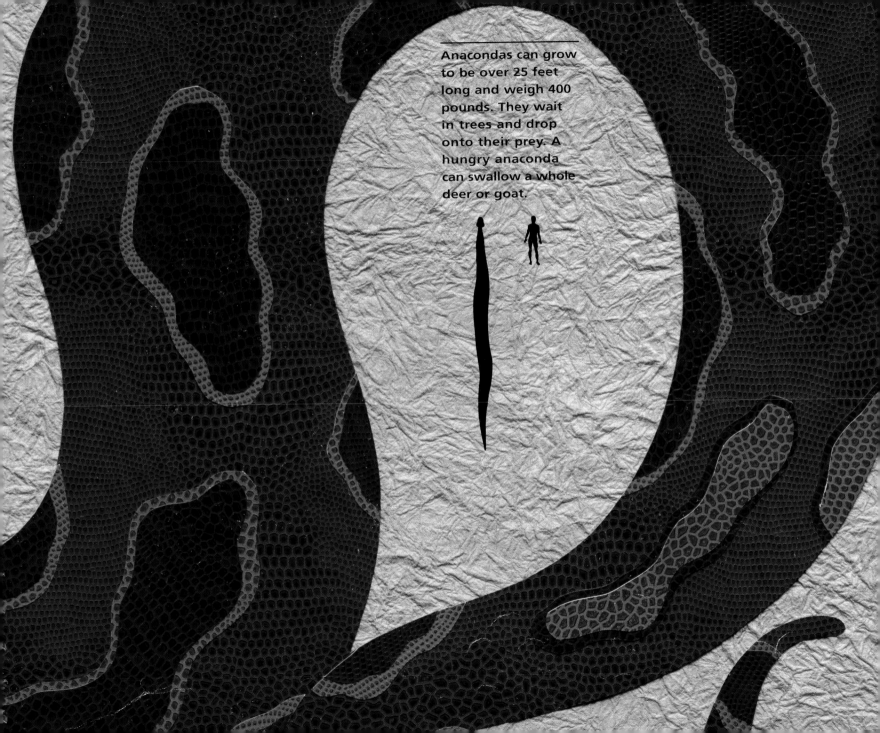

Anacondas can grow
to be over 25 feet
long and weigh 400
pounds. They wait
in trees and drop
onto their prey. A
hungry anaconda
can swallow a whole
deer or goat.

The flea is very small,
but it is the world's best jumper.

The flea is only 1/16 of
an inch tall, but it can
jump 8 inches into the
air. That is about 130
times its own height.
If a 5 1/2-foot-tall
woman could jump
as well as a flea, she
could leap to the top
of a 65-story building.

The Galapagos tortoise lives longer than any other animal.

Galapagos tortoises
can live to be over
150 years old —
about twice as long
as the average
person can expect
to live.

Animal	Record	Size	Diet	Range
African elephant	Largest on land	11 feet tall 13,000 pounds	Grasses, shrubs, tree leaves, bark	Central and Southern Africa
Ant	Strongest for its size	1/32 to 1/2 inch long	Plants, nuts, fruit, insects, small animals	South America
Giraffe	Tallest	19 feet tall 4,000 pounds	Leaves, bark, seeds, fruit	Central and Southern Africa
Blue whale	Largest	110 feet long 168 tons	Krill (shrimp-like animals)	Atlantic and Pacific Oceans
Etruscan shrew	Smallest mammal	2 1/2 inches long 1/25 ounce	Insects, larvae, lizards, mice	Mediterranean countries
Bee hummingbird	Smallest bird	3 inches long, 1/30 ounce	Flower nectar	Cuba
Sun jellyfish	Longest animal	Bell 6 feet across tentacles 200 feet long	Fish	Warm oceans
Bird spider	Biggest spider	3 inch body, 11 inches long with legs	Birds, lizards, large insects, small mammals	South America
Cheetah	Fastest on land	4 1/2 feet long (without tail)	Rabbits, antelopes, small grazing animals	Africa
Electric eel	Strongest electric shock (650 volts)	6 feet long	Fish and eels	Freshwater rivers of South America
Land snail	Slowest	1/4 to 2 inches	Algae, decaying plants	Every continent except Antarctica
Anaconda	Largest snake	27 feet long 400 pounds	Animals up to the size of a pig or deer	South America
Flea	Best jumper (130 times its height)	1/16 inch tall	Mammals' blood	Every continent except Antarctica
Galapagos tortoise	Longest living	5 feet long	Leaves, seeds, fruit	Galapagos Islands (off the west coast of South America)